7 Common Sense Factors To Avoid Being a Stupid Leader

*You Can Be a Smarter Leader—
If You Just Pay Attention*

By Tommy Gibbs

This book is dedicated to my good friend and mentor Thomas Johnson, who passed away at the young age of 42. Thomas's love, enthusiasm and passion for life, people and the automobile business was unsurpassed. Rest in peace Tommy Johnson.

ACKNOWLEDGMENT

A special thank you to Lance Helgeson, whose tireless effort of keeping me focused and on track made this book possible.

Contents

Contents

FOREWORD

It seems like every week a car dealer will ask me if I had read the latest Zinger e-mail from Tommy Gibbs.

The answer is always "yes," because Tommy's weekly e-mails have become must-read material for thousands of analysts, dealers, vendors and others who need to pay attention to current challenges and trends in used vehicles.

Tommy's got a unique knack for mixing the pragmatic and profound in his weekly e-mails. There's absolutely no question that Tommy has a deep understanding of the car business, and he's never afraid to poke hard at the assumptions, beliefs and practices that often keep dealers from realizing their full potential as retailers.

Maybe one of the most enjoyable parts of Tommy's weekly missives is the way he makes sometimes tough-to-swallow medicine go down easy. His writing reflects his character—a Southern gentleman who blends the right amount of charisma, charm and respect to tell it like it is or should be.

In other words, Tommy's weekly Zingers are must-reads for so many of us because they offer actionable, valuable insights that make a difference for dealers. For me and dozens of others, Tommy's e-mails are often the first thing we check in our inboxes on Wednesday morning.

I was glad when Tommy told me he was thinking about writing a book on leadership. As I'm sure you know, the shelves of bookstores and libraries are lined with books that offer guidance for aspiring business leaders. But I suspect there are few books that bring together the diverse mix of life experiences and wisdom that Tommy has collected as he's followed his heart and soul from one success to another, whether as a Marine, a college athlete, a high school football coach, an NCAA referee, a race car driver, a car dealer, or more recently, as a sought-after thought leader in automotive retail.

In each of these pursuits, Tommy's success owes to his natural ability to lead others. To see him in action is to witness a leader who makes the responsibility of properly inspiring, motivating and rewarding others appear easy.

With this book, I'm most impressed at the way Tommy distills the challenges of successful leadership to seven common sense factors. I think Tommy's spot-on in recognizing that, at its most fundamental level, great leadership boils down to doing a few things right at every opportunity.

As I read the book, I found myself thinking back to my own failures as a leader. I thought of several situations where, if I had applied the attention, empathy and introspection that Tommy discusses in the following pages, my decisions as a leader would have produced far more positive outcomes.

In the interest of full disclosure, I count Tommy among my closest confidantes and friends. I keep him close because his honesty, integrity and intelligence inspire me to be a better person. It's an absolute delight to see these same qualities come to life in a book that will make a difference for any aspiring leader who reads it.

– Dale Pollak, Founder, vAuto
and Executive Vice President, Cox Automotive

7 Common Sense Factors To Avoid Being a Stupid Leader

*You Can Be a Smarter Leader—
If You Just Pay Attention*

By Tommy Gibbs

The Stupidity Problem

I often see leaders at the highest levels of some of America's best businesses make dumb mistakes.

Let's call it the Stupidity Problem.

It's not that the people in leadership positions aren't smart. On the contrary, they're often some of the smartest people I've ever met. They know balance sheets. They know budgets. They know forecasting. They may even have a knack for strategy.

But here's the problem: Many of these leaders are absolutely stupid when it comes to leading people. It's amazing. Some of the smartest people on the planet turn absolutely inept when it comes to empowering and motivating their employees to higher levels of shared success.

I see this problem again and again—so often, in fact, I'm starting to wonder if these men and women take stupid pills before they go to work in the morning.

Maybe it's a bit of envy on my part, but I can't help but shake my head and wonder, how in the world did these people get to where they are today? I'll bet you've done the same thing.

You see, effective leadership of people isn't complicated. It's actually pretty simple and it's 99.9% about paying attention. It really boils down to being observant enough to recognize good and bad, and distinguish between smart and stupid decisions. I'd like to think of it as "peripheral observations."

I've thought a lot about what could be called the "stupidity problem" among business leaders today. If you break it down, I believe there are seven common sense factors that, if leaders endeavor to follow, provide a pathway for effective and inspirational leadership. This book dissects each of these seven factors.

> "What makes a good leader? Leaders have to walk it as they talk it in spirit and action to truly create a culture of success."
>
> – Rob Howe, AutoTrader.com

I wrote this book to help smart leaders wise up and do a better job of effectively leading their people and improving the fortunes of their businesses. There's no reason for smart leaders to make stupid mistakes that undermine the best interests and motivations of the very people who can help (and want to help) them be more successful.

This book draws a lot from my experience in the car business as both a dealer and, today, as a business coach and consultant. It also reflects my experience as a college athlete, a head football coach at a private military academy, an NCAA referee and a member of the United States Marine Corps.

Through all of these experiences, I've come to recognize that the "stupidity problem" is both persistent and pervasive in business, sports and life in general.

It doesn't need to be this way and, in fact, it shouldn't be—especially since effective, inspirational and motivational leadership isn't all that difficult. Yes, it takes a little more time and effort. Yes, it may require you to step outside of your comfort zone. Yes, it might mean a bit of an attitude adjustment on your part.

But let's be clear: Overall, it's pretty easy to be a good leader if you understand, embrace and make the common sense factors of effective leadership part of your day-to-day routine.

Of course, the converse is also true—it's pretty easy to simply carry on and remain among the ranks of leaders who suffer from the "stupidity problem," sometimes without even knowing it.

The good news for you is that you've picked up this book, and read this far into the introduction. You're already on your way to becoming a better leader, and getting a handle on the common sense factors that will take your leadership abilities, and your organization, to the next level.

Thank you for choosing my book. Now, go lead.

CHAPTER 1

Strategy: Setting It Right, Keeping It Right

I've learned a lot about strategy over the years.

Perhaps the three biggest lessons I've learned are these:

- First, your strategy won't work unless your organization and team fully buys into it. Even the best strategies fall apart when faced with inattentive and ineffective execution.

"The essence of true leadership is rooted in humility and the ability to develop followership by engaging the hearts and minds of those around you."

— Bob Aston, Towne Bank,
Chairman & Chief Executive Officer

- Second, your strategy can and should change. In business, none of us works in a vacuum. We're all subject to the ups and downs of the market, operational imperatives and other factors. In this ever-shifting environment, a "sacred strategy" is often too rigid to serve you well. In fact, a "sacred strategy" can easily turn into a losing strategy, especially for leaders who are too bullheaded, fearful or inflexible to recognize their strategy isn't working.

- Third, your ability to establish and execute a sound strategy depends on your ability and willingness to embrace your own advancement and reinvention as a leader. In short, you must develop and nurture a thirst for knowledge.

One of the pitfalls of business leaders and especially automobile dealers is they get locked into specific strategies with processes, pay plans, culture, selling systems, etc. They often see themselves as being committed to a selling strategy that is no longer effective. Just because you've always done it a certain way doesn't mean it will continue to work for you. *Change is good. When you are through changing you are through.*

A Quest for a Bottom-Up Strategy and Buy-In

In the mid-'80s, my dealership had started to make some real progress. We had what I considered a good plan in place, but we were still not close to our real potential.

I was running around trying to gain as much knowledge as possible about how to build an effective culture/business and pushing most of the ideas from the top down. While many of the ideas were solid, I just wasn't able to get the team onboard.

Who Do You Include?

Great leadership requires inclusiveness with the right people at the right time. Far too often, leaders don't follow the inclusive concept or they include the wrong people in planning and strategy sessions.

If you're a dealer and you're not including the General Manager in the decision-making process, you need to rethink it.

If you're the General Manager and you're not including the GSM and/or the Parts and Service Managers in your decision-making process, you need to rethink it.

If you're the General Sales Manager and you're not including the Sales and F&I Managers in your decision-making process, you need to rethink it.

As an example, it's not a good strategy for a dealer or GM to hire an F&I manager who will ultimately answer to the GSM.

Yes, you have the power to do whatever you want, but you could very well be making the wrong match. If the GSM is going to be in charge of the sales department then the GSM needs to be involved in the decision-making process, which would include, but not be limited to, decisions such as hiring and advertising. Sure, you should give it your blessing, but not dictate which decisions should be made.

This inclusion works both ways. If you're the GSM, you should be smart enough to run key hiring and other important decisions by the GM. To do anything less is just plain stupid.

You're not stupid...you're reading this book, which means you're smart.

I certainly knew the direction I wanted to take the team, but the execution wasn't there. The more I wrestled with our strategy and plan, the more I realized that my team's resistance was rooted in the way I'd developed our plan—namely, it was my plan, not the team's plan. It became more and more apparent that until the team owned the plan and the strategy, it was never going to happen.

Finally, one day this reality set in, and I decided to take action with something I'd been considering for about three years.

For whatever reason, I'd saved a clipping from a local newspaper about a team-building course run by the city of Chesapeake, Va. The article detailed a "ropes and initiatives course" that was much like the obstacle courses I'd encountered in the Marine Corps that were designed to build comradery and confidence—the course was in the woods and it featured tall walls and other barriers that leaders and their teams of eight to 12 people had to climb and cross.

"The vision to have a clear goal for your team, and the humility to adapt and change what you thought would work, but didn't."

– Bob Martin, Germain Motor Company

I'd kept the article in the top drawer of my desk. Every time I would get frustrated with the lack of teamwork and our strategy fulfillment, I would pull out the article and mentally threaten that I was going to take the management staff out to the course.

I finally decided to pull the trigger. One day, I told all the members of the management team to meet me at the dealership at 6 a.m. I instructed them to wear jeans and tennis shoes and told them we were going for a little ride.

Several managers asked me to explain where we were going and why, but I kept the cards close. I simply said that I thought we needed time away from the dealership to get more acquainted with each other as a group.

There were some "What's going on?" expressions as we arrived at a wooded area with picnic tables. We were greeted by the course operator Jeff Christian and two of his assistants.

Jeff took us through a series of ice-breaker games, and then moved us to the much more difficult obstacles. I remember one obstacle distinctly—it was roughly 60 feet tall, with a rope climb and a zip line. Just looking at this obstacle would scare the bejeebers out of you.

Now, my management team was like most—a mix of people who were old and young, some fit and some overweight, some who loved the outdoors and others who preferred more civilized creature comforts. Still, everyone made it through the course.

It was amazing to see those who needed less help lending a hand to their fellow team members. There was a lot of shared encouragement and energy—a strong degree of collaboration that I hadn't seen in the dealership.

In the end, my managers, despite their different backgrounds and roles in the dealership, all started to recognize each other as "real people." They understood that each person had a unique set of ideas and skills that, when combined, ensured everyone could successfully complete the course.

> "Great leaders teach others to fish."
>
> – Ronnie Dalleo, Vets Ford

I was so impressed with Jeff Christian's ability to convince my team that they could do anything that I eventually sent all of my employees to the obstacle course, and saw the same results. (Later, I partnered with Jeff and my business partner, Ashton Lewis, to set up a larger course on 100 acres that we used to train our employees and other businesses, including dealerships and franchise organizations like McDonald's and the U.S. Navy.)

After the obstacle course, I understood that I needed to channel the positive team-oriented outcomes we'd achieved into changing the culture and strategy at the dealership.

Again, I opted for an off-site retreat to accomplish this important work. We secured a rustic 4-H camping area near Wakefield, Virginia. I felt it was important to go primitive—no phones or TVs to interrupt our focus. We picked several people from each department to ensure a cross-section of employees.

I invited Scott Rigell, who was and continues to be a very successful Ford dealer in Norfolk, Va., and is currently a member of the U.S. House of Representatives, to speak to our group. He was known as a forward thinker and the architect of a successful dealership culture. I thought that culture would fit our organization.

Scott had a major impact. He helped change the way my team thought about their roles and responsibilities in the dealership and laid the foundation for us to

develop a shared, strategic game plan that didn't solely come from me.

Of course, I was leading the strategy-setting discussions. I wanted to make sure our shared plan reflected my goals for the business. In the end, my team wrote and owned our new plan. And, most important, they put the plan into action back at the dealership.

To this day, I count this example of shared strategy development as one of the most successful things I've done as a leader and entrepreneur.

The "What and How" To Successfully Achieve Your Strategy

Even if you've got a sound strategy, with organization-wide buy-in and execution, it's important to recognize that change is inevitable.

"Effective leadership means being a good listener who is able to lead by example and motivate those around him to be the best they can possibly be, no matter the position."

– Larry Dewing, Orleans Chrysler

In fact, it can be a fatal mistake when leaders fail to recognize this reality and their carefully laid strategic plan becomes static, a plan that's stuck in the mud.

Most leaders would agree that you need to know "What" you are trying to achieve and then you need to know "How" you are going to get there to ensure proper execution of your strategy.

Think of your strategy as the "What" and your team's execution as the "How."

Once you've established the "What," then the "How" becomes what's important. The problem often occurs as you start to go down the road of the "How." Frustration starts to build when the "How" isn't getting it done. This frustration then begins to create doubt about whether the "What" is doable. Not long thereafter, the whole thing begins to unravel.

So let's talk first about the "What." The "What" comes about because of a need or desire to implement positive change and improvement. The "What" is the ultimate goal—you must stay focused on the "What" even though the "How" may change.

For example, the "What" for a car dealer might be the need to generate $500,000 in gross profit a month to pay the expenses and make a tidy profit. In some ways, the "How" you get there is not all that important. You just have to get there.

> "An effective leader is someone who is encouraging, yet critical; effective without being oppressive; able to see the short and long-term pictures; and always is morally sound."
>
> – Bob Murray, Sunnyside Toyota

It may be that you rely mostly on your fixed operations to generate the greatest portion of the gross. That's fine. You certainly need sales to carry its share, but with strong fixed operations, you can make it happen with a clear focus on an area where you excel.

Here's another example of the "What" and the "How." The "what" is you need $200,000 a month in used car gross. It may be that you can sell 100 cars at $2,000 a car or you can sell 200 cars at $1,000 a car.

Different sets of circumstances and market conditions may cause you to focus either approach on "How" you achieve the "What." But remember, the "What" has not changed. You need $200,000 in gross. What changes is "How" you get there.

In today's business environment for dealers, there are so many factors that affect the "How" necessary to achieve the "What" you've designated for your team: staffing, inventory availability, lending conditions, competition and your market.

If you are having great success today in your dealership with a certain type of "How," that doesn't mean if you buy another dealership 200 miles away that your "How" is going to remain the same. It's pretty easy to establish the "What"; the hard part is figuring out the "How."

There is no 10-step process and/or concept that will work all the time. You must stay flexible and keep scrambling to figure out the "How."

If It Ain't Broke...

We've all heard the old adage, "If it ain't broke, don't fix it." Wrong...it should be, "If it ain't broke, break it, fix it and then do it again."

I remember in my early days of being a dealer I started to question what the heck we were doing. We were changing this and changing that. The reality is the things we were changing needed changing.

The rabbit we're chasing is always on the move. The business is on the move. You need to stay on the move.

> Look at two top companies in the world, Apple and Nike. They are always changing. Always trying to be better. They make the competition chase them. They are the chasee, not the chaser.
>
> If whatever you're doing ain't broke, trust me, it's either broke and you haven't figured it out yet or it's getting ready to break.
>
> Get ahead of the curve. Break it, fix it and get ready to do it again.

The "How" is always changing. If you get a certain "How" implanted in your mind and it's not working then you end up having great doubts as to whether or not the "What" can be done.

In my view, the "Hows" are nothing but little bumps in the road on the way to achieving the "What."

When you've taken the effort and time to map out a realistic, shared "What" for your organization, it's important to avoid letting the changing nature of the "How" get you off track. You just have to keep your thinking sharp to achieve the "What" that is necessary for your organization.

The Strategic Leader As Chief Learner

I often remind dealers and managers that you never get this business right. There is always something to fix and, whether you want to admit it or not, the ever-changing nature of business is likely one of the reasons leaders like being leaders. If you weren't being challenged it wouldn't be half as much fun.

For me, every challenge represents an opportunity to learn something new. And, the older I get, the more I enjoy the gift that allows me to view every challenge as an opportunity to learn and improve my thinking as a leader.

I've decided the next time someone asks me what I do for a living I'm going to tell them "I learn."

"To succeed as a leader, you must empower those around you."

– Stephanie Wilson, Alpha Media

That's what I really do. I'm always trying to learn something. My brain is constantly reviewing information either through reading, communicating with others or observing—no matter the source, my brain is constantly in "review and refresh" mode, like a mental hard drive.

This curiosity and desire to learn comes from a familiar place for many business leaders; I have a fear of being left behind and I don't like the view from the rear.

For some leaders, the appetite and hunger to learn comes easy. Oftentimes, these leaders were born with a keen curiosity and thirst for knowledge. Other leaders, however, aren't as blessed. They are often prone to "go with what they know" rather than pondering the possibilities that can come from applying new approaches and ideas to their business and overall operational strategy.

In working with these leaders, I've found that it's useful to review what are commonly known as the "Four Stages of Learning" to help them recognize the biases and traits that thwart them from becoming lifelong learners.

Here are these "Four Stages of Learning," plus two others I've developed that can help identify the learning stage(s) that applies to you and key members of your organization.

1. **Unconscious incompetence:** The individual does not understand or know how to do something and does not necessarily recognize the deficit. The individual must recognize his own incompetence, and the value of the new skill, before moving on to the next stage. The length of time an individual spends in this stage depends on the strength of the stimulus to learn. The more time he is willing to spend learning the skill or activity the faster he will move to the next stage.

   Example: You decide to take up golf, so you go out to the driving range and whack at a few balls. You make great contact on one out of every 10 shots, but you have no clue what you're doing. You know you love the feeling and you know you want some more of it, so you keep returning to the driving range and/or play a few rounds of awful golf.

   "There is NO 'Do as I say, Not as I do.' Lead by EXAMPLE!"

   – Michael Warren, Hendrick Lexus, Charleston

   ---

2. **Conscious incompetence:** Though the individual does not understand or know how to do something, he or she does recognize the deficit, as well as the value and necessity of acquiring new skills to address the deficit. The making of mistakes can be integral to the learning process at this stage.

Example: After going to the driving range for a while and playing a few rounds, you begin taking lessons with a pro and quickly realize how little you know. You observe others either at the golf course or on video, etc. The realization of how much you can learn about the game starts to sink in.

3. **Conscious competence:** The individual has developed enough knowledge and understanding to be competent with new skills and knowledge, but it isn't yet second nature. He must concentrate on single steps, with a lot of thought applied at each stage to execute a new skill or apply new knowledge.

   Example: More golf lessons, more golf rounds played and you are starting to understand the integral parts of the swing. You haven't mastered the swing yet, but you are starting to strike the ball more consistently, especially when you think it through. It's not automatic, but your skills are improving as your knowledge starts to grow. This can be the most frustrating stage of all. You still have to think about it. When you do, your results are much better and when you don't, you want to throw your clubs in the lake.

4. **Unconscious competence:** The individual has had so much practice with a skill or new knowledge that it has become "second nature" and can be performed easily. The individual may be able to teach it to others, depending upon how and when it was learned.

Example: You've now repeated your golf swing enough times, played enough rounds, attempted enough different types of shots that you can break par or better and have reached a very competitive level. You no longer have to think about the elements of your swing, you just do it. The physical and mental muscle memory is locked in.

5. **Competent Incompetence:** This is the most dangerous of the six learning stages. It's when you have years of experience, know your stuff and have become convinced you have nothing else to learn. Your success has convinced you that you are "the man," (or "the woman") and you are done learning. Seeking more knowledge is the last thing on your mind. You're a firm believer that what got you to where you are today will carry you forward.

Example: These individuals are easy to spot in leadership positions—they get defensive when anyone challenges their edicts and ideas. In the car business, it's not uncommon to see these competent but incompetent leaders as a key reason behind an under-performing dealership.

6. **Learning to be competent:** This stage never stops. It's a perpetual journey that keeps life interesting and challenging—and keeps your abilities and skills invigorated and sharp. For these individuals, learning is a journey, not a destination.

Example: Leaders who are constantly learning to become more competent will often have organizations that respond much more quickly (and positively) to change than their peers. In short, the leaders' ability to adapt to change, incorporate new thinking and master necessary new skills becomes part of their DNA for themselves and their organizations.

"Leadership needs boldness and compassion to be effective."

– Mary Cook, Bob Huff Chevrolet Buick GMC

As your journey continues to become a more effective, strategy-minded leader, I would ask you to identify the stage of learning that best fits you, and each of your top managers and team members. Who amongst you resists new ideas that might improve your business? Who seems to be making the same missteps time and again? Who prefers to "go with what they know"?

The answers to these questions—and the stage-of-learning exercise itself—will help you identify key aspects of your operation that may be impeding your ability to craft and execute the strategy that will take your organization to its next level of achievement.

CHAPTER 2

Discipline: An Essential for Effective Leadership

"Discipline yourself, and others won't need to."

– John Wooden

"He is disciplined…doing the right thing not some of the time, not most of the time, but all of the time."

– Former Chicago Bull B.J. Armstrong on Michael Jordan

"A good leader must be harder on himself than on anyone else. He must be disciplined himself before he can discipline others. A man should not ask others to do things he would not have asked himself to do at one time or another in his life."

– Vince Lombardi

If I learned anything from being an athlete and coaching various levels of baseball, basketball and football, it's this: It takes a well-disciplined team to win.

Now, some might disagree. They might argue that talent trumps discipline.

But it doesn't. Talent can combine to produce a winning team, but that team won't win as consistently or often as the well-disciplined team.

Over the years I've had the unique opportunity of hiring and working with some really talented people. I can tell you that, more often than not, it's not the talented people who are the most successful. It's the well-disciplined who succeed, time and time again.

Picking The Right Players

Great leaders know one of their most important contributions is picking players. Picking the right players doesn't mean necessarily picking the most talented. It means picking nice, coachable people who are passionate about what they are doing.

How many times in your career have you observed really talented people fall on their face? You've seen it in sports, business and the movie industry. Often in the car business they can sell the heck out of cars, but, but, but…their ego, their lack of discipline or some flaw causes them to crash and burn.

A leader's job is to slow the process down. Make sure the entire organization understands the culture, the mission and what type of team members have the best chance to succeed within the organization.

When you pick the right team members…they succeed…the organization succeeds, which creates powerful momentum. Momentum becomes a driving, motivating force to push on, doing it again and again, to create an unbeatable formula for success.

I had to let go one of the most talented individuals who ever worked for me for the simple reason he just didn't know how to talk to or treat people. He had an amazing amount of knowledge that was unsurpassed in the business, but I finally had to sever ties.

To this very day he continues to struggle. He's bounced from place to place. Always seems to get hired, but wears out his welcome very soon. I know you've seen people like this yourself. In the final analysis it always comes down to discipline and self-control.

The talented people possess a special gift, but they often lack the discipline to take their talent to the next level.

Signs of Poor Personal Discipline

A lack of personal discipline can show up in a variety of ways—here are some common examples I've seen over the years. Individuals who lack discipline:

1. **Cannot manage their personal lives.** They make bad choice after bad choice.

2. **Cannot manage their money.** If they can't manage their money, the odds are they can't manage your organization's money either.

3. **Cannot manage the truth.** They are not honest with your customers, your staff or themselves. They would rather take the easy route than the right route.

4. **Cannot manage their time.** If they can't manage their time, they sure as heck can't manage other people's time.

5. **Cannot manage their emotions.** They tend to talk down to people. They treat others—your staff and your customers—poorly. They may even be confusing their own lack of emotional control as "intensity," which becomes an excuse to act like a jerk.

6. **Cannot manage results.** They get results confused with doing it right. They think as long as they get the numbers it doesn't matter how they get there.

The problem is further fueled by upper management—leaders will often focus too much on the actual results as opposed to how the results are being achieved. In time, it all catches up and the real result is that due to a lack of discipline the organization suffers from chaos and, in some cases, may face legal issues.

Keys To Personal Discipline For Leaders

For me, personal discipline has become second nature. In addition to my time as an athlete and a coach, I served in the United States Marine Corps.

> "An excellent leader is someone who not only inspires, directs and manages, but also gets the most from his or her people by demonstrating, empowering and teaching those who follow."
>
> – Andrew Hermes, Deacon Jones Auto Group

The Marines are not a large branch of the military, and they are often the first into battle. The cornerstone of the Marine Corps and its creed is discipline.

The emphasis on discipline starts in the Marine Corps boot camp and it's a two-way deal. You have to be disciplined about doing your job and looking out for your fellow Marines—much like the discipline good coaches stress with the athletes on their teams.

The bottom line is, just as in sports and the Marine Corps, if you lack discipline, the odds of you being an effective and successful leader go way down.

So how do leaders make sure they have the discipline necessary to ensure the success of organizations, people and themselves?

Discipline is about doing the right things all the time. Discipline is about creating good, solid habits. Discipline shows up in many forms in the workplace including being on time, completing assignments, and dressing appropriately. It also shows up in the way you interact with other people—how you talk, what you say, how you say it and who you say it to.

I cannot fathom someone achieving a key leadership position unless they possess a high degree of discipline.

If you do not have a sports background, military background or if you didn't grow up in an environment where there was a focus on discipline, then you may be at a total disadvantage as you attempt to climb the ladder of success. It is virtually impossible to achieve success in sports or the military without discipline, and business and life are the same.

Take a hard look in the mirror. Is your personal life a mess? If so, it's pretty much a sure bet that the lack of discipline in your personal life carries over into your professional life. The chaos you feel on the home front may not be as dramatic as the chaos at work, but you can bet it's there and it's probably become your best friend.

Does Being On Time Matter?

I don't know if you follow pro football and it doesn't matter all that much if you do or don't. At the beginning of the 2013 season the Tampa Bay Buccaneers lost their first two games on field goals at the end of the game.

There was a bit of controversy about their quarterback Josh Freeman. At the time, Freeman was also the team Captain. After that, his teammates chose not to elect him back to that position. There was a rumor that the coach rigged the voting because the coaching staff had lost confidence in Freeman's play and leadership skills. I doubt all of that's true.

Then this lack of confidence was further magnified when Freeman overslept and missed the team picture.

I want this to be as simple as I can make it. Regardless of your skill level, regardless of your talent, regardless of your position, regardless of how much money you make, you cannot be a leader if you can't show up on time.

Discipline is about self-control. It's about doing the right thing when the wrong thing keeps screaming, "Why bother?"

Focus on improving your discipline, regardless of where you have come from and where you might be today. Observe others around you who you deem to be well-disciplined and start to emulate them. Pretty soon others will start to emulate you, and now the tribe becomes very powerful.

Only the best-disciplined individuals ever get to be the chief of the tribe. One of my favorite sayings is "The pain of discipline or the pain of regret." The beauty and curse of being a leader is you have the choice to pick your own path.

> "Leadership is the capacity to translate vision into reality."
>
> — Jesse Rowray, Jim Norton Toyota, Oklahoma City

I like to think of discipline as a "Some Will, Most Won't" scenario. This means if you have the ability to exercise more discipline in your personal and professional life, you have a huge advantage.

To its core, discipline is about making good decisions for yourself, your company and those you associate with—much like the players on a successful team or the Marines in a platoon.

Discipline also applies when you make bad decisions as a leader. The following exchange highlights how discipline can help make the best of a bad decision:

"Sir, What is the secret of your success?" a reporter asked a bank president.

"Two words."

"And, sir, what are they?"

"Good Decisions."

"And how do you make good decisions?"

"One word."

"And sir, what is that?"

"Experience."

"And how do you get Experience?"

"Two words."

"And, sir, what are they?"

"Bad decisions."

– Anonymous

CHAPTER 3

Empathy: A Powerful, Necessary Leadership Trait

Some leaders think it's better to be gruff and tough with their people.

They believe that showing empathy and understanding is a sign of weakness, and not a characteristic of an effective leader.

I feel bad for these leaders, because they've adopted a style of leadership that will not carry them very far—and they're missing one of the most basic and simple facts of human nature: People respond favorably and positively when a leader shows a level of empathy and understanding they did not expect.

The definition of empathy is the capacity to recognize someone else's emotions. One may need a certain amount of empathy before being able to experience accurate sympathy or compassion.

"If you want to know what a man's like, take a good look at how he treats his inferiors, not his equals."

– J.K. Rowling, Harry Potter and the Goblet of Fire

Some suggest that empathy is a character trait learned early in life, and one that is difficult, if not impossible, to develop later in life.

Years ago, I served as a referee for NCAA basketball games. For each of the 17 years I held the job, the

---

NCAA would hold a clinic for referees. Every year, the NCAA would bring in an FBI agent to speak to us about the hazards and temptations that might come our way and how to avoid them.

The conversation more or less revolved around the possibility that some fans, or even a group of fans, might try to put you in a compromising position to influence the outcome of the game—and protect the bets they, or their associates, had placed on a game. (During those years, betting on college basketball was greater than betting on professional football.)

I distinctly remember an FBI agent and former FBI Academy instructor tell us that people "are who they are" from about the age of five or six years old. He relayed stories about would-be FBI agents who, no matter how much instructors discussed the need for honesty, integrity and doing the right thing, would simply not "get" the message because they weren't taught those traits (or values) at an early age.

I tend to disagree with the FBI agent/instructor. I believe people can change; they can learn to be better individuals and manage how they react in specific situations. But they won't be able to achieve this transformation without first understanding the power of empathy and applying it to their day-to-day behavior and decisions.

I say this because I didn't embrace empathy myself in the past. But I got lucky: I had mentors who showed me how empathy can be a powerful tool for leaders to change behavior in an organization and get the results necessary for success.

The "People Skills Paradigm"

Famous last words, "I have great people skills." How many times have you interviewed someone and you ask them to name something they are really good at and they say, "I have great people skills."

I often ask that question of people I meet and then I'm amazed to learn they can barely spell "people skills," much less execute them.

Leaders understand that having great people skills requires them to grow those skills daily by building relationships of trust, respect and productive interactions.

Steven Covey stated it best when he said, "Trust is the glue of life. It's the most essential ingredient in effective communication. It's the foundational principle that holds all relationships." Having people skills means building relationships.

You may think you are a great people person, but if you can't be trusted then you're a long way from having people skills.

Having great people skills involves the ability to communicate effectively with people in a friendly, positive and uplifting way.

President Dwight D. Eisenhower said, "You do not lead by hitting people over the head – that's assault, not leadership."

In reality, these mentors were passing along an important leadership lesson they'd learned themselves, often from someone else. The following are some of the insights I learned from them, and feel privileged to pass along to you.

The First Rule of Empathy:
Stay Connected and Grounded

Not long after I had started my training business and it began gaining momentum, I had an opportunity to become a partner in a Toyota store in Chesapeake, Virginia, part of the First Team Auto Group.

The assignment was intended to be short-term—essentially to help pave the way for a talented GM within our organization who would take over the store.

I asked my assistant at the time, Martha Crawford, who still works for First Team, for her perspective on why the dealership became more productive and profitable in a very short time.

"Effective leadership happens when you've cultivated enough respect from your crew that they simply WANT to do tasks for you."

— Patrick Rawn, AutoNation Ford, White Bear Lake

"Whenever you visited the dealership, after running the store for only a few months, the whole place perked up," Martha recalls. "I will never forget that. You make people feel important, and, face it, everyone wants to feel important."

What was my secret for the success? I made a concerted effort to stay connected and grounded with everyone at the dealership. I took time with each individual team member to meet one-on-one and ask about their challenges, both on the job and personal. I also made a point of following up with other managers to fix issues employees raised that had a negative effect on their performance.

To this day, I'm convinced this daily exercise, which some might consider too time-consuming, is the number one reason the collective attitude of the team picked up and they immediately became more productive.

I should add that this one-on-one time with employees wasn't an original idea of mine. I learned it from mentors who taught me the power of empathy as a leader.

Over the years, I've learned that it's impossible to have empathy for someone as a leader if you don't create the opportunities for empathy to occur. For me, the one-on-one meetings created the opportunity, allowing me to stay grounded and in touch.

Therein lies a key problem for some leaders; they become separated from reality. They lose their empathy and feelings for the reality of the situation or the person at hand.

It's also true that as leaders go, so goes the organization. The more empathy a leader brings to the job, the more it will carry through the entire organization.

Empathy is one of those things that with the right mentoring can be learned, changed and improved. There is no substitute for good role models, regardless of your age or background. Are you setting the right example as a role model for those around you?

The Second Rule of Empathy: The "Golden Rule"

Perhaps the easiest way to make sure empathy is one of your leadership traits is to simply follow the "Golden Rule," or treat others as you would want to be treated.

The Problem With Power

"The two hardest things to handle in life are failure and success."

– Anonymous

Have you ever noticed that when some people get behind the wheel of a car, truck or SUV that they lose their minds? It's not unusual to see someone driving really nutty, doing something really stupid. You pull up beside them and they look like normal people. They don't have two heads, fangs, or horns sticking out of their heads.

What is it with people when they get behind the wheel of a car? Good people, nice people seem to go a bit postal. As I've mentioned in the past, I used to drive race cars. I always found it interesting that some of the nicest guys outside of a race car were nuts once they got in the car.

It was as if their helmets squeezed their brains until stupid flowed out. I'm not excluding myself from that equation, as I was no different than the rest when I strapped on my helmet. It's probably the power of the engine that makes them go off the deep end.

I see the same thing in business every day. Someone gets promoted and, BOOM!, they get the "king of the hill" mentality. "I'm 'da king, you 'da peasants, and you will do as I say." That type of mentality will soon be their downfall.

One of my father's favorite sayings is, "Be nice to people on the way to the top because you never know who you will meet on your way down."

By definition, this approach puts you in a position to understand what others are feeling because you share their experience and can put yourself in their shoes.

It's not unusual for those in leadership positions to respond negatively when someone disagrees with them. The disagreement is often viewed as the subordinate not respecting authority.

To understand empathy is to turn this thinking around and ask yourself, if you disagreed with your boss, does that really mean you are being disrespectful as long as you present your case in a respectful manner?

What if the boss went further and said, "Hey, you seem to have a problem with authority!" How would that make you feel?

It's often not easy to accept a differing point of view as simply that—another perspective. It takes a little time to think through what you want to say and how your comments will be received.

But showing empathy as a leader will often require that you have to push yourself to try to view things from the other person's point of view. You may not have thought of empathy as a vital skill of being a leader, but it is a powerful tool in leading, developing and building an organization.

"Effective leadership creates an environment of sustainable success."

— Lori Morris, Stanley Auto

The "Golden Rule" goes a long way to ensuring empathy is a part of your leadership skill set.

As I have matured as a leader (and you will too), I have come to believe that my ability to show a greater sense of empathy helps me to connect with others, remove barriers and accomplish far more than I might have in my younger days as leader when I didn't do so.

In some ways, the FBI instructor was right—those who learn early on about the power of empathy have an edge. But that's not to say that if you've had bad mentoring or parenting in the past that you are stuck. You can change your ways. The fact you are reading this proves you are seeking to become a better leader.

The Third Rule of Empathy: Be Wary Of "Lead Bulls"

There are times when showing empathy can be very difficult, especially when dealing with individuals with big egos—people I like to refer to as the "Lead Bulls" in an organization.

In James Michener's 1974 novel *Centennial,* he discusses the "Lead Bull" theory. The Indians had to kill buffalo and had to do it without modern day weapons.

To do so, they excited the herd so the lead bull would run toward a cliff. The herd would follow closely behind. Because the lead bull was running at such a frantic pace, he was unable to stop and the momentum of the following herd would knock him off. Because the lead bull "jumped" off the cliff, the other bulls simply followed.

> "Effective leadership is living, working and expressing your expectations."
>
> — Randy Guell, Holiday Automotive

At the bottom of the cliff, the Indians would finish off any animal not killed by the fall, and then they'd process each buffalo for food, clothing and other needs.

Joe Maddon, a former manager of the Tampa Bay Rays baseball team, has talked about how he used this method to move the team in the right direction. "The premise, in short, is to have the veterans lead the others in doing things the right way," Maddon says.

His point is that in the clubhouse (your business is the clubhouse), you have to get the lead bulls running in the right direction and by doing so the others will follow.

The problem in your business is often your "Lead Bulls" frequently want to run in a different direction. It becomes difficult to deal with them at the same time while showing empathy. The more they run in a different direction, the more disruptive it is for your younger, less experienced bulls. These lead bulls can really challenge the leadership empathy concept.

The danger here is that leaders can sometimes go too far trying to show empathy with lead bulls and look the other way. These leaders often justify ceding ground to the lead bull because of the results the individual produces.

You may remember Manny Ramirez who played for the Boston Red Sox and other Major League Baseball teams. Ramirez, though a great player, often did his own thing to the detriment of himself and his teammates. But, because he was such a good player, it was often forgiven by saying "That's Manny, just being Manny."

In the end, this empathy-driven "pass" tended to pull not only Manny down, but also his teammates.

"A good leader is one who praises his subordinates, appreciates his clientele and is never satisfied with his culture or process."

— Butch Tucker, Hutcheson Ford

The reality is that leaders can't afford to allow "Manny to be Manny" if they want to lift the performance of their entire organization.

Somehow, your job as a leader is to get the "Manny Bulls" to help lead the "baby bulls," or you'll have a whole house of "Manny Bulls" running wild.

The lead bull shows up in many places within a dealership. Furthermore, there is often more than one lead bull within the store and within the departments. It may be your top sales person. It may be your top sales manager. It may be your top technician. It may be your back counter parts person or it may be someone on the clerical staff. There are many lead bulls in any given organization.

Your job is to find them, seek them out, corral them, feed them, nurture them, and turn them into the lead bull they have the potential to be, not the lead bull they think they want to be.

Your best approach when dealing with the lead bull is to develop a one-on-one dialogue that allows you to appeal to the lead bull's ego. Let's call it working with "ego empathy."

It's important for you to acknowledge to the lead bull that you understand they are a natural leader, and that you need their help to get the rest of the team doing the things the organization needs to be successful.

The key words here are "I need your help"—they appeal to the lead bull's ego and underscore your empathy or understanding that this trait is important to your organization.

In essence, you're asking the lead bull to follow your approach and processes because of his or her responsibility to the collective team. Likewise, you're asking the lead bull to continue producing big results that can lift the performance of the entire group.

In such situations, the lead bull often responds positively because they recognize that their performance and role in the organization is valued, and they have a chance to further establish themselves as a leader. In a way, the lead bull has been tricked again.

Empathy is a good thing. Too much empathy is a very bad thing. Figuring out how to balance empathy without letting the lead bulls run wild is the key.

Don't think for one moment you will do a little dancing with the lead bull and they know the steps. The Lead Bull will follow you as long as you hold their hand. Turn the hand loose and they will go into dancing freestyle faster than you can yell "Geronimo!"

CHAPTER 4

Being Responsive: A Matter of Choice and Frogs

One of the great disconnects among leaders is the mindset that they don't need to be responsive to others—unless it's something they deem urgent in their own minds.

This approach misunderstands the expectations and intentions of the individual who asked for a response. For them, the leader's response is important, otherwise they probably wouldn't have asked for it in the first place.

"An effective leader is a person with experience who listens and then responds with common sense."

– Barry Moore, Haley Buick GMC

As a leader, if you receive an email, phone call, letter or text message, it should be handled in the most expeditious manner possible. There's a difference in just missing something and intentionally not reacting to it.

The lack of responsiveness goes even deeper when you tell someone you are going to do something and you don't. Be a person of action. Be a person of doing. Be a person of doing it now!

Many years ago, before technology became what it is today, FedEx would supposedly delay providing status updates on packages. When someone called about a package, FedEx would ask for their number and tell them they'd call back within five minutes with the information.

But FedEx had the information in hand—so why the wait?

The story goes that FedEx believed it was more impressive to call the customer back when they said they would than to actually tell the customer right away. We could debate that technique, but what we can't debate is the positive impact it had on customers. FedEx consistently did what it said they would do, and customers came to view them as a highly responsive organization they could entrust with their packages and shipments.

The same is true for leaders in any business. We get more respect and trust when we do what we say we are going to do, when we say we are going to do it.

Responsive Leaders Eat The Frogs First

I have always tried to live by Mark Twain's quote, "Eat a live frog first thing in the morning and nothing worse will happen to you the rest of the day."

Eating the frog first is a little known secret of top leaders. Smart leaders are responsive to those things that are the most unpleasant first. Getting the difficult task out of the way allows a clear path for a productive day. Hitting customer complaints and employee problems head on is the frog that smart leaders eat first.

I can tell you from personal experience I love eating the frog first. I always, always do those things first that I hate doing the most.

> "An effective leader is one who leads by example, inspects what they expect, has defined, clear processes in place and treats EVERYONE the way they would want to be treated."
>
> — Michael Finley, Peters of Nashua

Sometimes your frog is a customer complaint, an employee issue, or a major decision that needs to be made for the company that can only be made by you. The sooner you nail it down, the sooner you do it, the faster you get it handled, the more you will turn your day into a productive one.

What could be more impressive than someone requesting something of you (any message or communication with you can be considered a request) and you immediately respond? It often seems that those in a power position, manager or boss (notice I didn't use the word leader here) think that the world serves them. They believe that because they sit in the biggest seat, the peasants should come beckoning to them, and expect a response on their time.

Great leaders know they serve others; it's not the other way around. Serving others means being responsive to them. If someone in your organization needs to speak to you, it's your responsibility as a responsive leader to get back to them ASAP if you can't address their issue right away. Even if you know what the issue is and even if you don't want to deal with it...you must. It's another frog. You are the leader. You as the leader must set the example.

Are You "The Decider?"

Leaders like you make decisions. That's why you get to be the leader. You get paid big bucks to make good decisions. Embrace it, love it, groove on it. Be cool about it.

Isn't it amazing, then, how many people in leadership positions can't make a decision? They have to ponder every little detail, every little "What if?" There are very few decisions that require this much thought.

Your training, your knowledge and your confidence should be such that you do it, get on with it and if you screw it up, you fix it and move on.

Not being able to make quick decisions would be like a quarterback walking up to the line of scrimmage and thinking, "Now let me see, what could go wrong here. Should I do an audible? No, maybe I shouldn't. Wait...maybe I should? Nah, I really shouldn't, not this time anyway. I'll just run the play I started out with."

By the time this quarterback made a decision, the referee would call a delay of game penalty. Not only that, the quarterback's teammates would feel and see the hesitation, which would erode their confidence in him.

That's what goes on when the team knows you can't or won't make decisions. And when you do make a decision they have no confidence in you and the failure rate goes way up.

Knock it off. Make some decisions. Know your limits, and know when to ponder the few that need pondering.

In most cases, just "get it on," as in "I got this."

A Responsive Leader = A Responsive Organization

How can you expect others within your organization to be responsive to customers and teammates when they observe you doing just the opposite?

Leaders have to keep reminding themselves that they set the tempo/atmosphere for the entire organization. The leader's responsiveness will carry over in how the staff reacts towards customers and each other. If a leader doesn't see the need to be responsive, guess what happens to the level of responsiveness among managers and employees?

Over time, the lack of responsiveness will erode the organization's effectiveness and productivity—it will perform poorly compared to one where leaders set an atmosphere of responsiveness wherein everyone views themselves as equals on the same team, serving each other.

Breaking Resistance

Resistance is everywhere. It's all those people yelling at you that it can't be done. It's you thinking, "I could never."

You have faith in yourself. You know you can do it. But, resistance keeps yelling at you from the far left hand lower corner of your brain, "Have you lost your damn mind? You can't take such a chance."

Resistance is fear. It's you being scared. It's you being afraid to take a chance. But consider this:

Resistance is as natural as the sun coming up each day.

Resistance is you being afraid to swing from your heels and go for the fences.

If you're going to ever have your breakout moment.

If you're going to make it happen.

If you're going to climb the mountain.

If you're going to control your destiny.

If you're gonna kick ass and take names.

Amid all these ifs, at some point you need to tell resistance where to go and get on with it.

You're smarter than resistance. I believe in you. A lot of people believe in you. You believe in you. Let's go!

A responsive leader builds trust and respect minute-by-minute, action by action. This proactive emphasis on being responsive does two important things:

- It efficiently takes care of the requests for guidance and help.
- It sets an example for others.

When leaders create a culture of instant responsiveness, it catches on. Employees use it with their peers, and their customers. It creates an environment where everyone effectively says, "I know your needs are important," to each other.

It's also important for leaders to recognize that being responsive is not just limited to requests for your guidance or help. You must also be responsive to the needs of your business.

Here's an example from my days as a car dealer. Like the used car manager at most dealerships, my manager controlled a lot of money and a lot of inventory at any given time during the month.

The manager had the power to decide if/when a used car needed to be wholesaled. The used car manager makes this decision because some vehicles require too much money to be spent on them to retail, they have too many miles, or they are just a bad fit for the dealership and its market.

Typically, there are two used cars that managers decide to wholesale—units that aren't retail pieces and those whose life cycle has run out.

> "Effective leadership means trust—everyone you deal with MUST trust you."
>
> — Dave Kirk, Dave Kirk Automotive

No matter the car or its' life cycle stage, I made a point of being responsive to my used car manager's decision. I took time to evaluate every transaction once it had been completed.

I had two concerns as I evaluated my used car manager's decisions.

First, I wanted to make sure we weren't wholesaling cars that we could/should have retailed. Second, I wanted my manager to think like me—it was, after all, his job to maximize the investment of my money in every vehicle.

When those wholesale units came to my desk for review, I would call the used car manager and ask some specific questions about who, what, when, how much and so on. Regardless of the amount of loss or profit on a particular unit, I would ask, "Did we make the right decision? Is the unit in question a unit that we could have sold to a retail customer vs. a wholesaler?"

I would also ask questions to underscore my focus on the bigger picture—"Why are we selling so many cars to Bob's Auto Wholesalers? Could we have done a better job at the auction? Was this the best decision for this vehicle and the dealership?"

Some might think I was creating a situation where I simply second-guessed the used car manager. Maybe, but I'd rather think of it as a real and responsive way to ensure a good system of checks and balances, and a positive outcome for my business.

My responsiveness (and my questions) were intended to pass on my experience and perspective and, in turn, provide guidance to help the used car manager make better decisions for himself in the future.

The other real plus from this approach is that it causes the manager to become responsive, and their responsiveness begins to build within the organization. They become very influential as they start to read and act upon the request of the "leader." As they do so the leader sees them as growing, learning, paying attention and they therefore earn the trust and ear of the leader, who they actually start to influence. The end result is a "we're all in this together" environment, one that recognizes we must be responsive if we are going to achieve maximum results and success.

This is all well and good, except in those situations where a manager/leader is not responsive. If the leader is pushing helpful information out to management, and they choose not to react and/or learn then you may have an unresponsive manager. This casts a negative cloud on the organization.

You will often find the unresponsive manager is a power pusher. They push their perceived power toward the team, which creates mistrust, divides the team and kills the execution of the major plan. They create fear for those around them as they begin to fear for their own job. The team begins to doubt the power manager. The team sees the power manager as one who is only concerned about his/her self-interest vs. the team's interest.

Two-Way Responsiveness and Peripheral Vision

Responsive leaders are not just giving out responses, they are actively receiving and seeking. They look for them, they seek them, they crave them. They understand being responsive is a two-way street. I often refer to this skill as having early warning internal radar, better known as peripheral vision and peripheral hearing.

When I played college football I played defensive safety. In those days, the defensive safety needed to be one of the fastest players on the field. I wasn't very fast, but I was very quick. There's a big difference in being quick vs. being fast. As a leader in a business, it's essential to be quick and fast.

It wasn't my quickness that allowed me to excel in the defensive backfield. It was my "peripheral vision." I could see the entire field so well that very seldom did an offensive player get behind me.

"You know you're leading effectively when your associates enthusiastically follow your lead."

– Cary Donovan, Swope Auto Group

Having peripheral vision is something all great leaders either have as a basic instinct or they are able to develop over time. Leaders with peripheral vision have the ability to see things going on around them that others either don't see or just ignore. It allows them to be responsive.

It's virtually impossible to utilize peripheral vision when your head is stuck inside a computer all day long. Good common sense says that if you "ain't looking, you ain't seeing."

It's not just about peripheral vision. Great leaders have peripheral hearing. Peripheral hearing allows you to be responsive. Having the ability to seek out and listen to key people in your organization will improve the overall health of the company. You might think of it as a network of spies. It's not that at all. It's having an open line of communication with key staff members so you hear about situations before they become problems.

There are two major keys to peripheral listening. Never betray the confidence of the person who is attempting to help you and use the information wisely. At all times, this information should be used in a generic way, in a group meeting or one on one as an example of what goes on at other companies. There's a right way and a wrong way to make use of the info you've been entrusted with.

Once you've tossed it in the air, then you need to look and listen to make sure the proper action is being taken. If not, then you need to take additional steps to ensure the company's best interests are being served. As a leader, having great peripheral instincts isn't a luxury, it's a necessity. If you can't see it or hear it, you definitely can't fix it. And you'll never fix it unless you learn to become more responsive.

You can up your response skills and the responsive skills of the rest of your team by paying attention to what's going on around you. Look for opportunities to put being responsive into play. Sometimes it's the littlest things you do, say or react to, that can have the biggest impact on developing a team of immediate responders.

Being responsive is one of the most powerful, yet neglected, skills of those in leadership positions.

CHAPTER 5

Enthusiasm: Bring Meaning to Moments That Matter

"Enthusiasm is one of the most powerful engines of success. When you do a thing, do it with all your might. Put your whole soul into it. Stamp it with your own personality. Be active, be energetic and faithful, and you will accomplish your object. Nothing great was ever achieved without enthusiasm."

– Ralph Waldo Emerson

I can't imagine anyone being a real leader who isn't enthusiastic.

"Effective leaders have the ability to inspire above-average results from average people, with everyone moving in the same direction with a shared vision."

– Adam Britzius,
Lithia Chrysler Dodge Jeep Ram of Billings

Being enthusiastic means "getting after it." Enthusiastic leaders bring high energy and speed to each moment—a persistent pace, cut-to-the-chase conversations, rapid-fire thinking, quick responses, an ever-percolating sense of urgency.

I realize there are some very successful leaders who are anything but high energy or enthusiastic. But I have to believe that 99% of the world's great leaders possess this trait, or they can at least fake it. Enthusiasm is one of those things that sometimes you have to "fake it till you make it." If you act enthusiastic then you will eventually be enthusiastic.

When I started selling cars in the early '70s, one of my first mentors was Thomas Johnson. He was the General Sales Manager at Bill Lewis Chevrolet in Portsmouth, Va. Thomas hired me to join the sales team.

Thomas' best friend growing up was Ashton Lewis, Sr., my business partner for some 30 years, and the son of W.O. Lewis, the store founder.

Thomas' love of the business and zest for life goes further off the charts than I could ever describe in just a few words. He loved people and he loved getting after it.

He was special!!! Thomas passed away in 1989 at the very young age of 42. There are very few days that go by that I don't think of Thomas and the high degree of enthusiasm he brought to his life and work.

At times, Thomas's enthusiasm could seem bipolar—it could flash in a moment of temper but 60 seconds later he would have you laughing and ready to sell a car.

It was impossible to work around Thomas and not be able to feel his energy and excitement about the car business.

The Wisdom of "Whatcha Got?"

One of Thomas' sayings was "Whatcha got?" As in why are you standing there? What can I help you with? Are you selling a car or what?

Thomas was a firm believer in making sure each sales person knew they were the most important person in the world. His goal was to get salespeople to understand he'd drop everything for them and, in turn, they would do the same for him.

When a salesperson walked in the tower (the sales manager's office) and there was a conversation or phone call underway, everything stopped. The next thing you'd hear was Thomas asking, 'Whatcha got?'"

To this very day, I follow that same drill.

"The best leaders inspire the people around them and lead by example."

— John Fabre, Infiniti of Baton Rouge

If I'm doing consulting work in a dealership and I happen to be in the sales manager's office having a conversation and a salesman walks in, the first thing I say is, "Hey, whatcha got?" My goal is to set a two-way example; for the sales manager, it's "Let's take care of him first, we can talk later." For the salesperson, it's "Our stuff can wait. What do you need because you're the most important person in the world at that given moment?"

How Hot Are Your Tires?

I know a little about NASCAR racing, not a lot, but a little. Believe it or not, I've raced late model stock cars and modified cars. Ain't no rush like it.

Did you know that the air pressure in the tires starts low at the beginning of the race to allow them to expand as the race gets going and the tires heat up?

The tire size and air pressure is also different on each side of the car. The inside tires (the left side) are smaller than the right side tires to help the car turn through the corners.

You may have noticed that when a caution flag comes out during a race you will see the drivers weaving back and forth before the green flag comes out. They do this for two reasons: To get debris off the tires and to maximize tire heat and expansion, which is even more important. The moral of the story? You have to keep the heat in the tires if you wanna go fast.

It's the same deal for leaders. You have to keep the heat on. But this doesn't mean beating people up. If you put the heat on in the wrong way, you will lose a lot more than you win. When done correctly and in the right situation, keeping the heat on is a good thing.

I can remember going on appraisal rides with Thomas. It wasn't at all unusual for us to make a quick detour to a McDonald's, where Thomas would pick up 30 cheeseburgers and 30 French fries. Back at the dealership, he would start handing them out to an appreciative (and hungry) team. Yes, Thomas could even make cheeseburgers and French fries exciting.

Thomas' enthusiasm was egalitarian. He could get just as excited about meeting a new team member as he could if he met the President of General Motors. He loved the big guys and he loved the little guys.

How Enthusiasm Drives Extra Effort

Insights on Inspiration

"A mediocre person tells. A good person explains. A superior person demonstrates. A great person inspires others to see for themselves."

– Harvey Mackay

1. **Challenge with reasonable objectives.** Not too easy, not too hard. The key is they have to be achievable. Tossing out "pie in the sky" numbers doesn't challenge people; it defeats them.

2. **Lead from the front, push from the rear.** Cheer and cheer some more. There's nothing better than a pat on the back or a double high five to get 'em going and keep 'em going. Sometimes you have to show them "how" and sometimes you coach them "how."

3. **Watch what you say and how you say it.** Saying the right things, in the right way, at the right time can do wonders. Choose your words carefully. Remember the whole world is watching and listening to everything you say and do.

4. **Show you care in a sincere way.** It has to be real. There's nothing more powerful than a leader that truly cares. You can't fake it.

Being enthusiastic and energetic as a leader creates a positive effect on all team members across all areas of your dealership or business.

Back in 1991, we hired a young man by the name of Travis Sullivan to clean cars. After a couple of years, he became our prep manager or, as some might say, the reconditioning manager.

Historically, the dealership clean-up/prep guys hold lower-paid positions, and it's not uncommon for them to leave not long after they're hired. This makes the manager's job difficult because you're often dealing with quality control and production issues—problems that don't go away if you're constantly bringing new people on board.

But Travis turned the operation around. It was truly amazing. He was able to hire better quality people, and he set high expectations for their performance and work quality. I'm convinced that Travis' level of energy and enthusiasm allowed him to achieve stellar results. His people would constantly go the extra mile—in part because he expected the same from his people as he did from himself.

One of my worst decisions ever was to go into the motorcycle and watercraft business. In that business you are often buying units based on "the come." You order units in the winter that you hope you will sell by the end of the summer. One year we had about 20 watercraft left over from the summer season. I asked Travis to clean them up and store them in an empty service bay we had available. Travis and his team not only cleaned the 20 units, they also bubble-wrapped each one.

I didn't ask Travis to do this. He could have cleaned them, moved them to the service bay and be done. But, instead, Travis went the extra mile by going to the trouble to bubble-wrap them.

While this might seem like a small thing, it's indicative of the power that energy and enthusiasm bring to an organization—a lot of "small things" add up to a very big, positive result.

As a leader, it's your job to be on the lookout for these little things and take the time to acknowledge the people like Travis in your organization.

Beware The Signs of "False Enthusiasm"

We can all agree that we need more Thomas Johnsons and Travis Sullivans in our organizations.

But there's a downside. We often have people who are just the opposite—They simply don't have it. It's what we might call "false enthusiasm."

"An effective leader is someone who leads from the front. They always practice what they preach in all aspects of their position, while empowering and mentoring those they lead to handle challenges on their own."

– Larry Preddy, Action Automotive

False enthusiasm is dangerous for any business. It often hides and lurks under the guise of Lip Service and Loyalty.

These individuals can sometimes be difficult to identify. They are often long-time employees who show up for work every day, but that's about as far as their work ethic goes. As leaders, we sometimes mistake this diligence to show up for work on time as loyalty.

But these individuals are often those who pay lip service to leadership directives. They are the ones who say, "Yeah, yeah, I get it. I understand and will make the necessary changes." They are saying one thing and doing another. Their heads are shaking yes, but their minds are really saying "no way."

As a leader, it's your job to try to remedy what these individuals might be lacking—and do so with enthusiasm.

In many cases, the inability of these individuals to meet your organization's expectations and performance standards is similar to the way "bad muscle memory" hinders some individuals from excelling in certain sports.

Knowing, Loving, Believing

You can't fly into Oklahoma City and not notice the awesome statue of Will Rogers sitting on his horse, lasso in hand.

I often see quotes by him and I'm always amazed at his wit and smarts that to this day remain true. Rogers died in 1935 at the young age of 55 in a plane crash in Alaska. The more I read his material the more brilliant I think he is.

Here's a typical Will Rogers quote: "If you want to be successful, it's just this simple. Know what you are doing. Love what you are doing. And believe in what you are doing."

Leaders know what they are doing because they are students. They always seek a better way because they know they never really get it totally figured out.

Leaders love what they do because they are passionate. It's important to understand that this love and passion may have been inspired by someone or something else.

Leaders believe in what they do because they know what they are doing and they love what they do. They seek to serve those around them through stewardship of their knowledge and passion for those things they believe in. What could be more powerful than sharing knowledge, love and beliefs?

Think of sports where good muscle memory is essential for peak performance:

- Shooting a basketball
- Throwing a baseball
- Tossing a football
- Swinging a baseball bat
- Hitting a tennis ball
- Swinging a golf club

The action of doing these is based on muscle memory. As time goes on, it is extremely difficult to make changes to any of these actions due to old muscle memory.

The key for sports coaches, or business leaders, is to provide the opportunities and training for employees to undue the "bad muscle memory" that can hinder optimal performance—while recognizing that this transition takes time to occur and, quite honestly, it may never happen for some people.

And it's these people who are most likely to be the ones saying, "Yes, yes, now I get it," while their on-the-job performance suggests this isn't the case, even when you've invested time and effort to help them improve.

When this situation occurs, it's essential that you do not make the mistake of rewarding lip service with undeserved loyalty.

The dictionary defines loyalty as "being faithful in allegiance to one's lawful sovereign or government; faithful to a private person to whom fidelity is due; faithful to a cause, ideal or custom."

But your business is neither sovereign nor a government. It is not a person, a cause, an ideal, or a custom. It is a business, where real results matter.

We all go to work each day, and we are expected to put out our best efforts and use our talents to their fullest. Perhaps we are even expected to serve above and beyond the call of duty (or at least beyond what we feel our current pay justifies!) In turn, we expect a fair wage, or at least an agreed upon wage. This is where loyalty begins and ends. If the level of service that employees give the organization doesn't meet the grade, the company's obligations end there.

An employee is not disloyal to a dealership if they fail to do their best; they would be disloyal to themselves. And if a company retained an employee in spite of mediocre performance just because he or she has 20 years of supposedly "loyal service," it would actually be disloyal to other employees and the stockholders.

Leaders who bring energy and enthusiasm to their organizations are often able to recognize when "false enthusiasm" occurs. They also recognize it's sometimes necessary to part ways with employees who, despite their lip service, do not meet the performance standards you expect.

While these situations can be difficult, they are not a burden for enthusiastic leaders. Rather, they are simply part of the necessary evolutionary process that helps an organization and its people improve.

CHAPTER 6

Articulation:
A Lack of Articulation
Leads to Evaporation

As a leader, it is impossible for your team to be successful if your message and the organization's message are not clearly articulated.

Some leaders sort of know what they want from their teams, but they cannot communicate the message effectively enough for it to settle in and drive desired behaviors.

"Effective leadership is the ability to convey a vision to the point where others take action to achieve the defined objectives."

— Ken Wright, Lithia Motors

Time after time, I have observed organizations develop a well thought out strategy, game plan, new culture, company philosophy, or guiding principles. It looks good on paper and sounds good in principle.

In practice, the new initiative falls flat. Why? Oftentimes, it's because the leadership team did not clearly articulate their mission and performance expectations.

A Valuable Lesson

I learned a very valuable lesson about communication early in my career while running my first new car dealership.

Every day, we held a morning meeting. We would review the forecast and compare it to our current standing on the daily operating controls (DOC) sheet.

We had a large white board that showed each day of the month. Each day showed the forecasted projection of individual department sales. At the meeting, each department head, in front of the rest of the leadership team, had to post their actual results.

After this exercise one morning during a difficult month, I told the department heads:

"If you have staff members who are working here who are unhappy, then they should go to work someplace else. If they are unhappy, they are doing themselves, the customer and their teammates a disservice by staying here."

My purpose, of course, was motivational. I wanted my managers to light fires under the poor performers in their departments.

> "You must have a vivid goal, and then share it, teach it, map it, modify it when needed, practice it, and repeat it every day."
>
> – Bijan Fathi, Stanley Direct Auto

But my service manager, who was new in his position at the time, took the message literally. He went straight downstairs to the service department and called everyone into a meeting.

He told the advisors and technicians that I had effectively laid down a new law, 'If they weren't happy working here, their ass needed to hit the street.'

Obviously, that's not exactly what I said, and I spent the rest of the day meeting with each service department employee to let them know I valued their service, but our collective performance needed to improve.

The lesson? Shame on me for not articulating my point more clearly.

Mastering A Collective Mission

It's extremely important that leaders clearly communicate a collective mission that encompasses the organization's core values, vision and actionable objectives.

This statement says a lot, but it essentially means that the best organizational mission statements actually reflect the organization, not just its leadership.

In the early '90s, my dealership was struggling with who we wanted to be as a company. In other words, our mission needed some refinement.

Scott Rigell, who's mentioned in the first chapter on Strategy, and I collaborated on holding retreats at the 4H facilities in Wakefield, Virginia.

Both of us believed that our new identity and mission would work best if it represented a cross section of ideas from everyone, rather than something we dreamed up in the Ivory Tower.

How Good Is Your Stuff?

Are you giving good stuff, bad stuff, outstanding stuff, worthless stuff, amazing stuff, same old stuff? Are you giving your best stuff?

So really, what is it?

Great leaders understand the power of giving. They give their best performance every day and they give back to others. They don't hide their stuff. They put their best stuff on the table to share with others. They share stuff that makes others have better stuff. Then they teach others to share their stuff.

It's full circle. Someone gave to you. Now it's time for you to do the same.

We brought questions for our teams to answer collectively. We used the answers to write a collective mission statement. Here are some of the important questions that led to a lot of insightful discussion and sharing:

1. Who are we?

2. What are we about?

3. What are our core values?

4. What's our mission statement?

5. How can we be better?

6. What's important?

7. Why do we come to work each day?

To this day, I'm convinced that the collective mission we developed—which emphasized a collaborative, fun work environment with an emphasis on customer service—led to happier employees and, in turn, happier customers. Even better, our culture became well-known around town, and we'd often find ourselves fielding inquiries from employees at other dealerships who wanted to work with us.

Our success was owed to an understanding that each employee had a personal stake in the company's mission and they understood that as we satisfied customers, the dealership would prosper and there would be more opportunities for everyone.

Avoid The "Evaporation Factor"

Whatever an organization's message or mission might be, it has to be constantly reinforced to be effective.

> "Great leaders are easy to get to when someone needs help or answers to a question, which helps everyone stay focused on the same goals."
>
> – Ed Johnson, Fred Beans Automotive

In my workshops, I talk about the evaporation factor. I don't care how good you are, what business you are in or how well disciplined you and your team might be, the sense of a collective mission, and the processes you build to support it, will tend to evaporate.

When this evaporation factor occurs, it's often due to organization leaders taking their eyes off the ball. They forget that it's their job to constantly communicate and reinforce how and why the organization's day-to-day processes actually empower employees to achieve the collective mission.

Some leaders take this responsibility very seriously, because they understand the evaporation factor lurks right around the corner if they take their foot off the gas pedal.

For many years, Dave Mullen served as the GM of JM Lexus in Margate, FL. Previously he had worked at Automotive Profit Builders (APB) near Boston. In fact, Dave helped implement the APB selling system, which includes a greeter/up, at our dealership in the early '80s.

While Dave worked at JM Lexus, the dealership consistently sold 750 new units a month, while doing $1,000,000 a month in service gross profit. Even now, those are amazing numbers; back then, they were nearly impossible to believe.

I had to know how Dave did it. One day, we were in a meeting and I asked him, "Dave, I'm in total awe of these numbers. I wish I could think this big but I'm having a hard time wrapping my head around 750 new units and $1,000,000 a month in service gross.

"A great leader is someone who walks the talk, who communicates the vision well and who has heart."

– Laurie Johnson, Del Grande Dealer Group

But, what I'd like to know is what do you do when you come to work each day to run such a massive and successful operation as this?"

Dave paused for a moment and offered this: "Tommy, when you are selling this many cars you're going to have a few unhappy customers, so the first thing I do each day when I come to work is to put out a few fires, take care of the 'heaters' (or what I call the 'frogs'). But, I see my real job here is to do one thing and one thing only and that is to guard the processes."

That's when I understood the connection between day-to-day processes and the organization's mission.

You see, Dave knows that the processes want to evaporate and he has to stay on top of them to ensure the evaporation doesn't occur. He also understands that staying on top of the processes requires constant articulation of what's important with every team member.

Dave made this a part of his daily routine. He was in the dealership all the time, keeping a watchful eye for instances where a process fell short and evaporation might take hold. He understood how critical it was to nip the evaporation factor in the bud to avoid bigger, more persistent problems.

A clearly and consistently articulated organizational mission is critical to a leader's success and ability to avoid the evaporation factor.

If you aren't good at articulating your message and mission, it's a skill you can learn. A good technique is to try to put yourself in the position of those with whom you are trying to communicate. Seek to understand their point of view before you have the conversation. This simple step will go a long way towards articulating the right message at the right time.

Avoiding "E.D."—Execution Dysfunction

Having the ability to articulate the message doesn't ensure that the leader and the team will be successful. Many leaders and team members have E.D., "Execution Dysfunction."

> "Leadership—it's being able to take people in the direction you want them to go."
>
> – Michael Barlow, Wade Ford

It's one thing to have a plan, an idea, a goal, an objective, a vision and a totally different thing to execute it. To quote Thomas Edison, "Vision without execution is hallucination."

Here are some fundamentals that will help the best of articulators execute their plan and avoid E.D.:

1. **Get "buy in" from staff members:** Nine times out of 10, E.D. happens when staff members don't get a real sense of commitment from the top. They hear you say it, but they don't see you live it.

2. **Create Accountability:** You need to have systems in place to measure what's supposed to be taking place. Even more important, impose penalties if the measured targets are not achieved.

3. **Kill the Cancer:** There are always naysayers, people determined to undermine any changes you bring to the table. Negativity is like a cancer that will destroy the health of your business, and there comes a point where you have to cut out the cancer if the rest of the body is to survive and thrive. There are some people you need to replace and you must have the courage to do so.

4. **Properly Train and Re-train.** If you think you can put a process in place, train the staff and walk away, you are dead wrong. Training or coaching has to take place every day to reinforce continually the processes that help the organization achieve

its mission. Indeed, some aspects of training should take place monthly, quarterly or annually. But far too often business leaders want the "shake and bake" method—shake it up, put it in the oven and that's it. You have to be willing to train and allocate a certain amount of resources for continual training. In addition, you have to recognize that training never ends, and its' redundancy has a purpose. It's impossible to get everything right 100% of the time.

5. **Develop Your Own:** Although it can be very challenging and difficult to do, in the long run, developing your own sales organization is the most solid approach for consistent, long-term growth. Surrounding yourself with a team that is sold on the culture and mission of your organization is far better than continuing to trying to fix bad habits developed by those who have bounced from one organization to another.

This is the way CarMax operates. CarMax doesn't hire anyone who has ever sold a car before. When they open a new store, they promote from within and start the whole process over again, training the new people on their mission and way of doing business. If you are ever going to grow and remain successful, you have to develop your own staff.

"Effective leadership is always giving clear and accurate instructions that are easily understood."

– Billy Hobbs, Hutchens Chevrolet

---

6. **Celebrate Success:** Look for opportunities to applaud people and their "wins." I don't mean just a pat on the back. Maybe it's the employee of the month. Maybe it's a lunch party for the office staff for closing the month out after a hectic last minute rush. Maybe it's a record month in widget sales. Doesn't really matter. Find a reason to celebrate.

7. **Employees are More Important Than Customers:** It's a fact. If you want happy customers, you have to have happy employees. To strike this critical balance, you need to touch the heart and soul of your employees.

8. **Have a Sense of Humor:** It's OK to laugh at yourself. If your organization has gotten to the point where no one feels like they can laugh and smile, you will have some very miserable days ahead. A lot of miserable days is a formula for failure.

Remember: E.D. is no joke. You can have the best ideas, the best mission and the best processes. But if you don't have a solid plan of ongoing execution, it's all an exercise in futility. You, as the leader, need to be the guiding light for the committed, trained, positive people who buy into your message and mission, and help you execute the processes necessary to achieve success.

CHAPTER 7

Humor: Humor Makes Good Leadership Better

"Against the assault of laughter nothing can stand."

— Mark Twain

If you're in a leadership position or hope to be so one day and you don't have a sense of humor, then I suspect you take yourself way too seriously.

"We feel a fun atmosphere builds a strong sense of community. It also counterbalances the stress of hard work and competition."

— Elizabeth Sartain, former Chief People Officer, Yahoo!, and Vice President of People, Southwest Airlines

---

I realize there are people in top leadership positions who don't have a sense of humor, but I have to believe that, by and large, they are totally miserable people and not nearly as successful as they and their organizations could be.

As a leader, it's your responsibility to create a workplace that's well-disciplined, functional, effective and a fun place to work.

Some leaders believe that displaying a sense of humor means a lack of seriousness or discipline about the work at hand.

But I believe a leader's ability to laugh a little and show a sense of humor means the individual is real, spontaneous and, at any given moment, has the know-how to inject humor and lighten the joint up.

In my experience, working in a place of business without a sense of humor is like working in a room with the lights off. Humor turns the lights on and adds an immeasurable element to the organization.

"A sense of humor is part of the art of leadership, of getting along with people, of getting things done."

– Dwight D. Eisenhower

Back when I was running my dealerships, I personally conducted cultural training to make sure every team player knew the mission and what my leadership team expected of them. I was quick to point out that if they didn't have a sense of humor then our organization was the wrong place for them to be working.

I put it this way: "If you can't laugh at yourself, then you're going to be miserable here. So, it might be best if you make some plans to meet some new people at your next workplace."

To me, this was an important point to convey to my employees. It let them know that while I was serious about the business, I was also human and approachable.

And guess what happens when a leader demonstrates he or she is approachable? It's like a chain reaction— good ideas come to your table, the organization becomes more successful and the organization's success encourages other people to want to work for you.

It would stand to reason if everyone is walking around with a frown on their face in a stuffy work atmosphere then it's anything but upbeat. When you add humor, people are far more likely to be creative, which leads to greater production.

So go ahead, laugh at yourself and with your team. It's OK. It really is. And you, and those around you, will be better off for it.

Humor Appeals To Customers, Too

It's been said over the years that the best way to have happy customers is to have happy employees.

"Happy employees are more for quality and outcome. They create an atmosphere that reduces conflict and turnover, which makes customers satisfied and happy."

— Abe Bakhsheshy, Director of Customer Service, University of Utah Hospital

---

You've probably heard this saying, but you may not be aware of the reasons it's true. Consider what happens physically when you and your customers share a laugh:

It lowers the blood pressure. This doesn't mean that if you laugh all day, you can eat deep-fried bacon-wrapped Twinkies for dinner every night. But it does mean that a shared laugh between your employee and a customer will take the edge off a tense situation.

It reduces stress. While laughter helps lower blood pressure, it also eases the stress levels your customers might feel. If your organization's culture includes a lot of smiles and humor, chances are better than good that customers sense it, and their stress levels diminish.

One of my all-time favorite employees was, and still is, Jeff Waugh. Jeff has an Eddie Murphy-style horse laugh. With Jeff's humor, it's impossible not to like him. I've often said it's hard not to like someone who can make you laugh.

Jeff was one of my top-performing people, and I'm convinced that his easy laugh helped him connect with customers and give the organization a greater level of productivity than many of his peers.

"Fun doesn't stifle, it encourages depth and breadth among work relationships."

– Lee McGrath, Cambria Consulting, Inc.

When I took over my first car dealership in the early '80s, I made a decision to test how much humor might help us sell more vehicles.

We'd tried a "normal" dealership TV campaign, but we weren't getting the buzz or new business we thought we should.

"I'm much more productive when I'm having fun. The work just flows."

– Sandie Tillotson, Founder, Nu Skin

I borrowed a page from Cal Worthington—an iconic West Coast dealer whose 30-year run of TV commercials always included his dog, Spot. But the dog was never a dog; it was often an exotic animal, like an elephant or tiger, which Worthington would lead around with a leash during the commercial.

Worthington was highly successful, so I thought we'd give his style of humor-based, animal-aided advertising a try.

We started with a goat (which looked too much like a dog on TV), tried a hog (way too smelly and snotty for a comfortable shoot) and tested live chickens (far too much poop to clean up between takes).

In the end, I became the "Chicken Man."

This was a stretch for me. I'm a dark suit, long sleeve, white shirt sort of a guy—a style I'd adopted years earlier after reading the "Dress for Success" book. Yet, our new ad concept called for me to put on a chicken suit and go on TV.

The campaign and concept turned out to be a big winner. The chicken and I became instant celebrities in the communities we targeted with the advertising in Virginia's Hampton Roads area communities, which includes Virginia Beach, Norfolk, Chesapeake, Hampton and Newport News.

To this day, if you mention Parkway Pontiac Volvo to anyone who was around in the early '80s, they'll likely remember the Chicken Man ads.

We did some pretty crazy stuff with the Chicken Man. My trusted and awesome assistant, Martha Crawford, would write out some very funny skits using all sorts of crazy characters from Batman to Mister Rogers.

These commercials were either so bad, so funny or so amusing that people simply paid attention to us. Good, bad or ugly, the Chicken Man ads helped us cut through the clutter, which is never easy to do when it comes to TV advertising.

I believe the success of our Chicken Man ads is proof positive that humor sells.

"When work is a pleasure, life is a joy! When work is a duty, life is slavery."

— Maxim Gorkey, Russian writer

I think it's fair to say that all business organizations are striving to find that distinct difference that may matter most with their customers and employees. I suggest that as you develop your culture and share it with your community, make sure that humor is at least a part of the equation.

You don't necessarily need to launch your own Chicken Man campaign, but your customers and employees should readily be able to recognize that you and your leadership team are likable human beings with the capacity to laugh and smile.

Chances are, it'll be good for business.

Staying Smart—9 Common Ways Leaders Fail

Leaders make mistakes. It's inevitable because, like you and me, they are human.

But a mistake is different than a flat-out failure. You can fix mistakes. A failure, by contrast, suggests a deeper, more ingrained problem.

> "Great leaders hire, train and motivate people to attain their best."
>
> – Steve Emery, NADA

I've studied failures of leadership and, time and again, I see common reasons why a leader didn't last long, or lost the respect of the organization. I compiled the following list of nine ways leaders often fail to help you stay smart—and avoid the stupidity that undermines effective leadership.

1. **They have followed the lead of bad mentors.** There's an old saying about parenting—that kids "live what they learn." The same is true in business, and especially in the car business.

   It is not at all uncommon for sales and service managers to emulate whoever managed them as they came up through the system. This emulation is natural and part of the laws of nature.

But here's the problem; too many managers in the car business find success and believe "this is the way." They cling close to the style of leadership they learned, because it brought them success in their careers. In a way, they've been brainwashed to believe their way is the only way.

Unfortunately, this "stick to the script" style of leadership doesn't really work in the car business, or any business for that matter.

Over the years, I've hired managers who came with a reputation for making things happen. They had a strong track record of selling cars or generating customer pay work in service, which I took as a positive reason for bringing them to my team.

Of course, these managers didn't last very long, and it was my fault. I didn't do enough due diligence to determine if a manager's style of leadership would truly mesh with our culture and organization. I learned the hard way that these managers' successes were directly proportional to the amount of screaming, yelling and intimidation of employees, even customers, they deemed necessary to achieve success.

The lesson here is two-fold. First, smart leaders know how to separate the good leadership skills and traits they have absorbed from the bad. They never forget that "what got me here isn't necessarily going to keep me here."

> "I haven't found a better definition of leadership than John Maxwell's: 'Leadership is influence... nothing more, nothing less.'"
>
> – Bill Marsh, Bill Marsh Auto Group

Second, as a leader hiring new talent, it's critical to determine a potential manager's adaptability and style as a leader before you offer the job. It can be tricky because references may come from the very individuals who taught the manager how to lead. I like asking "What would you do?" scenarios to scope out a potential manager's leadership, creativity and flexibility, as well as their style. I've also learned that if the answers don't indicate a good fit, chances are better than good it won't be.

2. **They don't pay attention to what goes on around them.** When I was a defensive back in high school and college football, I was known for being a pretty fast player with great peripheral vision—someone who could "see" the field.

I have no doubt that my peripheral vision was my biggest asset as a player. It helped me make plays where good reflexes or speed simply weren't enough.

The same is true in business and leadership. The best leaders have excellent peripheral vision. They are constantly able to pay close attention to what goes on around them. They are always looking, listening and "seeing" what's happening in their organization.

As a player, part of my ability to focus and "see" the field was innate; and part of it was coached and self-trained to make it second nature.

"The use of consistent, calculated actions that may contain risk but provide an opportunity for all to succeed through accountability and accomplishment while sustaining the earned trust and respect of your team."

– Clark Henkel, Beck Toyota

Nine times out of 10, a leadership failure can be traced to a lack of attention or focus—for some reason, the leader stopped paying attention, if only for a moment.

Leaders who achieve this higher level of attention and awareness inevitably have fewer problems to address, and a higher level of success. Why? Because they're able to "see" potential issues arise, and address them before they've become more serious problems.

3. **They find change too challenging.** You often hear a business leader say one of the following:

- "If it ain't broke, why should we fix it?"

- "We've always done it that way so why change?"

- "We're not too good working outside our comfort zone."

I call a leader's "comfort zone" the easy chair of ultimate failure. Smart leaders are never comfortable and you shouldn't be either. The warm and fuzzy feeling inside the comfort zone often occurs right before the big slide to failure.

Great sports coaches are always looking for the competitive edge. Great business leaders do the same.

Great coaches and business leaders never allow themselves to stay in their comfort zone because they recognize that getting comfortable is one step closer to failure.

4. **They Lack The "Leadership Touch."** Here are comments you'll often hear about great leaders:

"He always remembered my name."

"He could relate to anybody."

"It always seemed like he cared for us."

Such comments happen for good reason; the leaders made it a priority to keep in close touch with their team members.

"Great leaders have the ability to positively influence the behavior of those essential to the completion of a desired objective."

– Bob Hembree, Bob Hembree Chevrolet

The opposite of this is pure poison for a good leader and his/her organization. It becomes all about them. They are the alpha and the omega. They eat first and would never eat last. They have "arrived," and the rest of the world is on standby. They stay locked in the ivory tower and, when they do come out, their noses are so far in the air they'd drown in a downpour.

Selfish and arrogant leaders have concluded it's all about them. They have the answers and are the smartest people in the universe. Their over-inflated egos and vanity become an incurable disease. They are always right and never wrong, and will soon fail.

These leaders have difficulty controlling their egos. Everything is about them. The only letters they recognize in the word "humble" are "me." They have a narcissist streak that keeps them excessively preoccupied with personal adequacy, power, prestige and vanity.

Such individuals perform well, but at what cost to the organization? Nothing turns people off like arrogance. There's a huge difference between being confident and being arrogant.

Confidence comes from being a student of your business and knowing what you are doing. Arrogance comes from being stupid and not being respectful of others.

Much has been written about "management by walking around," and there is a lot of truth in that statement and concept. Smart leaders stay in touch with their organization and its people by walking around.

When I was a dealer, I started every day by walking the dealership. My first stop was in service, where I'd take a moment and talk to each technician, and service writer. I'd then move to the parts department, the back office and, finally, the sales department.

Depending on the day, this took 30 minutes or so. The conversations weren't long, but they were personal. We talked about children, hobbies or what they did over the weekend.

My employees learned as much about me as I did about them. I also found that the more I kept in touch, the more willing my employees were to do what was right for the business, our customers and each other.

Great leaders understand that they don't have to be liked, but they do have to earn the team's respect. You can't earn this respect by staying in your office. Employees are quick to recognize (and often reject) the selfish and arrogant leaders who are out of touch with the organization and focused solely on themselves.

5. **They believe they have all the answers.** Time and time again, if I ask successful leaders for the key to their success I'll get the same answer, "I hire the right people."

By the "right people," these leaders are really saying that they hire people who are smarter than they are.

Such leaders don't have to be the smartest person in the room. In fact, they prefer if they aren't the smartest in the room because it gives them an opportunity to potentially expand and shape their thinking as individuals and leaders.

Put another way, these leaders are keenly aware that they "don't know what they don't know," and they take steps to minimize the areas where their insight or intellect may be lean.

> "A good leader has the ability to have people follow their lead and implement the processes they expect."
>
> – Jim King, NADA

The best leaders are smart enough to know they don't have all the answers. They are on a mission to learn from the best, seeking out groups and organizations of like interest where they can learn best practices and get insights to shape their own ideas. (In the car business, I highly recommend industry 20 Groups as an almost sure-fire way for leaders to gain knowledge and insights in an environment where they won't be the smartest person in the room.)

This quest for knowledge helps explain why these leaders succeed—they put learning, growing and personal development at the forefront of their lives.

By contrast, less successful leaders often need to be the smartest person in the room, and they are more resistant than receptive to new ideas and new ways of thinking. The "right people" for them are often those who won't question their decisions. These leaders inevitably end up operating in a custom-built cocoon that's often impenetrable from the outside. They will invariably end up less successful than leaders who constantly scan the horizon for inspiration and intelligence to make themselves, and their organizations, better.

Several years ago, I observed the failure and fallout that occurs when the "right person" didn't get his due at an organization because the leader was convinced he knew all there was to know about everything.

The business leader had brought on a new partner with the intent to train this individual to take over the active management of the business. On the surface, this seemed like a match made in heaven—the business leader had picked someone with a different and more diverse background, an individual who brought a unique set of ideas and skills to the table.

The problem? The business leader was so strong with his opinions and perceived knowledge that they bordered on intimidation. He acted like he was the "wizard" of the business to such a degree that the partner eventually had enough and gave up on the idea of taking a more active role in the business.

"The best leaders lead by example."

— Mike Porro, Sam Swope Honda World

The partner has since gone on to be very successful in a different business where, ironically, he now trains a future generation of leaders. Meanwhile, the business leader's organization continues to plug along. I can't help but think how much better the business would be if the partnership had a chance to come to fruition and the business leader had a better understanding that what he didn't know could actually hurt his prospects for success.

6. They lose their Integrity Compass. The integrity and credibility of an organization flows directly from its leader.

In the consulting work I do with dealers, I will sometimes see signs that the organization's leader has lost his/her integrity compass.

These signs can be small—promises that "I'll get back to you" or "I'll call you back" that are never kept. In my experience, such broken promises amount to simple little lies that undermine the integrity of the entire organization.

Think about it; if the leader isn't setting the example of keeping his/her word with employees, what kinds of broken promises or little lies are being told to customers?

I've also seen organizations where the leader's loss of integrity leads to bigger problems like stealing. This stealing may be as simple as fudging expense accounts or having a staff member cut his lawn on company time. Or "cutting the cake," which means the used vehicle manager and a buyer split the cash skimmed off a wholesale deal.

The lack of integrity on the part of a leader is corrosive to the overall organization. Team members recognize leaders without integrity quickly as they observe the leader saying something one way and actually doing something another.

> "Great leaders are assertive, organized, and involved persons who really show a passion for their craft with a willingness to get their hands dirty. This person will push their employees further than they ever thought possible."
>
> – Tyler Thomas, First Team Auto Mall

In these organizations, it's really only a matter of time before results become more important than how the team achieves those results. It's never surprising when I find these same organizations plagued by high levels of turnover and an inability to consistently attract people of high character and integrity—probably because these individuals are smart enough to recognize or sense a bad situation.

7. **Their passion slips.** I'd be a mega-millionaire if I could find a way to put passion in a bottle. It wouldn't take much to market the stuff to leaders who feel like their passion for their businesses had hit a dry patch.

Unfortunately, you can't put passion in a bottle, much less sell it. Passion comes from within and, I almost hate to say this, I believe that while everyone has the capacity for passion, there are far fewer people who learn how to keep their passion alive.

Let's think about relationships for a moment. It's inevitable that the passion between a husband and wife will have its ups and downs. The most successful couples, however, learn to recognize when they've hit a low point.

And what do they do to rekindle the passion? They focus their energy and efforts on the things they like and love about the other. They plan a getaway just for themselves. They find baby-sitters to take the kids so they can go out with friends and enjoy their company.

The same thing is true for great leaders. When the passion slips for these leaders, they look for ways to rekindle it. They challenge themselves and others around them to seek the next level. They become the kings and queens of tweaking things from great to greater.

Being better and getting better can become a fuel for eliminating passion slippage. There is no substitute for passion. How's yours?

8. **They socialize with the same subordinates too frequently.** A friend of mine relayed this story. He was an up-and-coming manager at a small publishing company. There were three other managers at a similar level of responsibility and tenure with the organization.

Over time, he felt like the company president gave more attention and direction to his fellow managers. "It was like he was playing favorites," my friend recalled.

I asked my friend if there was any reason to think this might be the case. "Well, they all play basketball together at noon every day, which probably has something to do with it."

My friend hit on a problem that often undermines a leader's credibility—socializing too frequently with the same crew of subordinates. It's impossible to manage and exercise fairness and discipline to all when a leader puts friendship above credibility. Even if a leader could actually separate the personal and business relationship, damage is done because of the perception of the rest of the team of favoritism and cronyism.

Perception is a powerful word. If I perceive you are a jerk, you are a jerk. It is not up to me to change my perception of you; it is up to you to change my perception.

Leaders can easily create the wrong impression when they become too friendly with a select few among those they supervise. Even if the leader isn't playing favorites, the perception is there, and it kills the leader's ability to connect and grow others who are outside the circle of the chosen few.

The lesson here is fairly simple. If you're a leader who likes to connect in a personal way with team members outside the business setting, ask yourself whether this fraternization is creating a perception that you might be playing favorites.

"Effective leadership is knowing how to apply one's personal momentum in a way that improves the momentum of others around that leader."

– John Warren, Rebbec Motor Company

Incidentally, my friend's time with his basketball-playing colleagues was short-lived, and the same pattern followed when the leader hired a woman as his replacement who also didn't play basketball.

9. **They don't develop other leaders.** While it's absolutely critical that leaders continually seek to improve their own abilities and skills, they have an equally important responsibility to make sure their team members do the same. Leading a business isn't like being an elected leader of government, where leaders often serve their terms and let the next elected official pick up the reins where they leave off. Instead, it's the obligation and responsibility of business leaders to develop leaders within their ranks, to prepare the next generation to lead the business forward.

But this obligation and responsibility to develop future leaders often goes unaddressed and unattended by current business leaders. It's easy to spot the signs of this leadership failure—the current leaders insist on making every decision (which is distinct from affirming, blessing or reviewing decisions made by subordinates), even down to the tiniest ones that have little or no direct impact on the organization's success.

The best business leaders recognize that their success is enhanced and expanded as they teach others how to lead and do things not just as good as, but even better, than they might have done themselves.

In my experience, the failure of leaders to develop other leaders in an organization often owes to a sense of fear and insecurity on the part of the leader. They're afraid that an up-and-coming leader will one day take their place, so they (knowingly or not) do things to protect their turf.

The problem is that this self-centered style of leadership ultimately hurts the development, growth and success of the organization. Sales and productivity will never be as good as they could be in these businesses, and there's a greater chance the organization itself may eventually implode when the current leader loses energy, focus or steam to do everything he or she considers his sole responsibility.

Great leaders, like great coaches, know their #1 objective is to teach. In business, leaders must teach the next generation of leaders what it's like to make important decisions and take on additional responsibilities—to fully understand their role as part of the future of the business.

The sad reality is that leaders who lack the ability to develop leadership skills in their team members are the ones who are constantly looking for the next lieutenant. Why? It's because they've once again lost someone to another organization that offered a better opportunity to grow and become a leader.

The easiest way to avoid this leadership failure is to remember this one-liner: If you ain't teaching, you ain't leading.

Tommy's 20 Questions
Good Leaders Ask Themselves

1. How much do I know?

2. Am I still learning?

3. Can we do it better?

4. Am I doing all I can do?

5. Am I restricting the team?

6. Am I giving the team the things they need to get the job done?

7. Am I seeking input from the team?

8. Do I love what I'm doing?

9. Am I being "loyal foolish?"

10. Has my thinking gotten stale?

11. Is the old way the best way?

12. Am I leading from the front?

13. Am I pushing from the rear?

14. Am I investing in myself?

15. Am I investing in the team?

16. Am I penny wise and pound foolish?

17. Am I hiring the wrong people?

18. Do I believe in what I'm doing?

19. Am I micro-managing or am I being a good "checker?"

20. Am I living on an island with a closed mind?

Tommy's 14 Things
Good Leaders Always Say

1. I need your help.

2. What can I do to make your job easier?

3. What do you think?

4. We can fix this!

5. How are you? (And mean it.)

6. Let's get our heads together!

7. I trust your good judgment.

8. You're the best!

9. Let's make something happen!

10. You rock!

11. It's not a problem, it's an opportunity.

12. Gimme a high five!

13. Love 'ya.

14. Whatcha Got?

Tommy's 10 Tips
To Sharpen Your Leadership Skills

I like to read about leadership. Over the years, I've read a lot of books from business leaders and coaches sharing their perspectives on what constitutes great leadership. The following list of 10 tips is based in part on the take-aways I gathered from learning what I can about the ways good leaders become great leaders:

1. Embrace Anxiety—It's motivation to take action.

2. Get after it—Focus your energy on making positive change. Crank up the intensity and aggravate the competition.

3. Put fear into perspective—What's really the worst that can happen?

4. Be ready—Preparation breeds confidence.

5. Don't dwell—Forget minor setbacks. Learn, and move on. Don't let the setbacks become the standard.

6. Maintain a healthy discontent—Be aware of people/things that block your progress. (Surround yourself with losers and you will continue to lose.)

7. Be wary of satisfaction—If you don't set the example and step it up, who will?

8. Avoid paranoia paralysis—Show others how to claw or climb out of an unproductive rut.

9. Always look for answers—Continual improvement doesn't have a finish line.

10. Never ever give up—Other people want to see you fail. Don't let others control your thinking.

Tommy's Top 40 Leadership Traits

I've said it before and I'll say it again: Becoming a good leader is not all that hard. It's a matter of paying attention to a lot of little, solid, fundamental habits and traits.

Below are 40 fundamental traits of great leaders, which everyone should seek to emulate regardless of his or her position on the totem pole.

1. Leaders have pep in their step.

2. Leaders are disciplined.

3. Leaders arrive early, stay late.

4. Leaders have a sense of humor.

5. Leaders are consistent.

6. Leaders follow the Golden Rule.

7. Leaders don't put themselves above others.

8. Leaders don't show favoritism by hanging out with subordinates

9. Leaders can be counted on.

10. Leaders answer their own phone.

11. Leaders return phone and email messages promptly.

12. Leaders dress the part.

13. Leaders respect others regardless of position or social status.

14. Leaders say thank you…a lot.

15. Leaders cut through the chase; get to the point.

16. Leaders listen because they know others have great ideas too.

17. Leaders understand the word "We" vs. the word "I."

18. Leaders pull others up not put them down.

19. Leaders don't work in fear of their jobs; they coach people "up" to take their jobs.

20. Leaders do what they say they will do when they say they will do it.

21. Leaders pick up after themselves…and others.

22. Leaders know what they know and know what they don't know.

23. Leaders take the blame when something fails and they give others credit when it works.

24. Leaders communicate then communicate some more.

25. Leaders help establish vision and direction.

26. Leaders remove obstacles interfering with production, not create them.

27. Leaders attack a problem now, rather than letting it grow into a cancer.

28. Leaders seek ways to simplify, not complicate.

29. Leaders seek knowledge, they learn, then they coach others.

30. Leaders make the tough decisions now, not later.

31. Leaders don't tolerate a fearful workplace.

32. Leaders are enthusiastic.

33. Leaders set the accountability standard.

34. Leaders have controllable passion.

35. Leader detest the statement "we've always done it that way."

36. Leaders accept mistakes as a part of forward progress.

37. Leaders see a problem as an opportunity to "fix it."

38. Leaders guard the processes but recognize when they are not working.

39. Leaders are optimistic realists.

40. Leaders lead from the front and they push from the rear.

Tommy's 21 Tips
To Help You Get Noticed

I'm often asked by managers and others what it takes to be successful in business and how to move to the next level. They will often imply that they do a good job, but feel frustrated by the lack of forward progress.

Doing a good job doesn't ensure you of anything except you get to keep doing a good job…until someone else comes along who can do it better and then you may be looking for another job that you can do a good job at. It takes more than doing a good job to get you noticed and to the next level.

21 Tips For You:

1. Come early.

2. Stay late.

3. Come to work to work.

4. Stay busy.

5. Seek information and education.

6. Understand you are owed nothing.

7. Do more than you are asked.

8. Be tenacious.

9. Steal someone's ball and run with it.

10. Force the passion. You may not be in the perfect job or perfect place. It's up to you to make it the perfect job at the perfect place.

11. If you do these things, someone will notice.

12. If you get noticed, you have a ladder to the top.

13. If you don't get noticed or this isn't the place for you, then you are developing some skills that will eventually get you noticed.

14. Do it at the next place and the next place until you get noticed.

15. Be so good that you can't be denied.

16. Pull others up and you will go up with them.

17. Set an example for others.

18. Get up, walk around, be nice.

19. Be enthusiastic, even on your worst day.

20. Dress up to the next level. Don't dress like the rest.

21. Your answer to the question, "How are you doing?" should be "I'm living an amazing life."

Tommy's 11 Ways
To 'Do More' Every Day

My business partner for over 30 years, Ashton Lewis, Sr., taught me some of the best leadership skills I could ever have hoped for.

Ashton taught me nothing is more important than always doing more. More than is necessary, more than is fair. When in doubt as to whether you've given enough, give some more. Here are 11 ways successful leaders do more everyday:

1. They do more than they know is necessary.

2. They do more than they know is fair.

3. They do more because it's the right thing to do.

4. They do more not expecting anything in return.

5. They do more even when they know it still may not save the day.

6. They do more even when they know it may not save the customer.

7. They do more because they know it's a teaching moment.

8. They do more because they don't want to leave this earth owing anything.

9. They do more because they can.

10. They do more because they see the big picture.

11. They do more because if not them, who? Maybe you!

Tommy's 12 Burdens (Opportunities) of Leadership

Evan Longoria is an all-star third baseman for the Tampa Bay Rays. Having been an excellent player for a number of years he has become their leader both on and off the field.

In a recent article he and former manager Joe Maddon discussed some of the burdens Evan faces as the leader of the team. I've never thought of leadership as carrying burdens; I'd rather think of it as the opportunities of leadership:

1. Being up when you are down.

2. Picking others up when they are down.

3. Doing the right thing when it's easy to do the wrong thing.

4. Being respectful when your instinct is to do the opposite.

5. Getting after it when you feel drained.

6. Making changes when staying the course is comfortable.

7. Doing what you have asked others to do.

8. Speaking softly when you'd rather make a lot of noise.

9. Making a lot of noise when you'd rather speak softly.

10. Showing up early when you know you can come in late.

11. Making tough decisions that others can't and won't make.

12. Delegating authority so others may learn and grow.

What great opportunities you have as a leader.

About the Author

Tommy Gibbs spent countless hours as a teenager, working at his father's used car dealerships in Richmond, Virginia, scrubbing engine blocks with Ajax and wondering how he might make a brighter future for himself.

At 17, Tommy spent a summer vacation working as a salesman at a Mercury dealership in Richmond. It was the mid '60s, and the car business was pretty much the Wild West. There were few laws to protect consumers, and even fewer rules at the dealership. Tommy saw first-hand how customers were essentially forced to sign blank contracts and salesmen told customers they had to buy a car because their vehicle, which sat hidden behind the building, had been "sold."

It wasn't a glamorous upbringing, and Tommy saw little in the experience to fuel any desire to be in the automobile business.

But his formative years did ingrain an ethic of hard work, and a never-give-up attitude.

These characteristics, as well as a knack for leadership, helped Tommy become a stand-out athlete in high school and college, where he played football, basketball and baseball. His on-the-field achievements as a defensive safety on Ferrum Junior College's national championship team of 1965 earned him and his team a place in the school's football hall of fame.

Tommy went on to study sociology at the Virginia Commonwealth University, which he attended while serving in the U.S. Marine Corps Reserves and working two jobs as a recreation center coach and overnight attendant at a gas station.

After college, Tommy spent two years as a physical education instructor, head football and basketball coach at Frederick Military Academy, Portsmouth, Virginia. As Tommy recalls, "I loved the job but I wasn't making any money and wasn't smart enough at the time to see the financial rewards of moving on to the college ranks."

This realization led him back to the car business. Like so many others, Tommy considered this choice as "something to do until something better comes along."

Tommy's work ethic and care for customers proved a successful combination as a salesperson at Bill Lewis Chevrolet in Portsmouth, Virginia. He quickly rose to the ranks of management, becoming the used vehicle manager at the dealership.

Within a few years, he accepted an opportunity to join his friend and mentor, Thomas Johnson, as the General Manager of a small Lincoln/Mercury dealership in that same city.

Tommy's desire for greater success led him to a sales opportunity with the F&I products and training company, ADR, where Tommy became the company's top trainer and eventual vice president of sales operations. "During those years, I learned a lot about what not to do when you're trying to run a successful business and lead people," he says.

In 1980, the retail car bug bit again. Tommy accepted a leadership position in Ashton Lewis' dealership organization. As a partner, Tommy went on to operate a number of successful dealerships, earning a reputation as an astute leader of people, results and innovation.

Due to the combination of difficult economic conditions and poor new car brands, Tommy focused on used cars as a means to survive. "We didn't have a choice," Tommy says. "It was either do a better job in used vehicles or find another line of work."

Tommy's understanding of the used vehicle business, honed through his early experiences working at his father's used-car lots, helped him successfully pioneer the concept of "total" dealership profitability.

Since selling his interest in the dealerships some 13-plus years ago, Tommy has devoted his time to sharing his business management and leadership development skills with dealers across North America. A hands-on consultant and trainer, Tommy spends the bulk of his time working shoulder-to-shoulder with dealership owners and managers, helping them improve their organization's performance, profitability and productivity.

Though Tommy's recognized area of expertise is the automobile business, his emphasis is always on helping leaders implement cutting edge ideas, technology, and processes through the use of leaderships skills that create *buy in rather than buy out.*

Tommy shares his insights through weekly newsletters that reach thousands of leaders inside and outside the automobile business. His purpose: Engage and remind leaders of what's important, what's right (not who's right) and what they might have forgotten.

Tommy is also an in-demand speaker at dealer Twenty Groups and the National Automobile Dealers Association (NADA) convention, where he has consistently earned top rankings from standing-room only audiences.

Through all his work in business, as well as his pursuits as a coach and NCAA college basketball referee, Tommy has learned that success will only follow when leaders create a culture and environment where it can flourish.

This book is dedicated to helping leaders recognize that the "u" in success is really all about you—that is, who *you* can influence, who *you* can positively affect and who *you* can inspire to reach the next level and beyond.